✹

For my father,

RALPH HYAMS

(March 27, 1913–March 26, 1998),

whose spirit I salute

with vodka, yellow roses,

and cinnamon toast.

✹

Copyright © 2001
CHRONICLE BOOKS LLC

All rights reserved. No part of this book may be reproduced in any form
without written permission from the publisher.

TEXT BY
Gina Hyams

PHOTOGRAPHS BY
Masako Takahashi

DESIGN BY
Alethea Morrison

MANUFACTURED IN CHINA
Typeset in Clarendon, Buckeroo, Berthold Bodoni, and Adobe Wood Type

ISBN 0-8118-3051-9

Distributed in Canada by
RAINCOAST BOOKS
9050 Shaughnessy Street
Vancouver, B.C. V6P 6E5

10 9 8 7 6 5 4 3 2 1

Chronicle Books LLC
85 Second Street, San Francisco, CA 94105
www.chroniclebooks.com

DAY OF THE DEAD

BY GINA HYAMS

photographs by Masako Takahashi

CHRONICLE BOOKS

SAN FRANCISCO

Table of CONTENTS

7
Introduction

11
Origins of the Day of the Dead

19
How the Holiday is Celebrated

55
Traditional Recipes

69
Creating Your Day of the Dead Home Altar

89
Suggested Reading List

91
Acknowledgements

*"Day of the Dead celebrates
the intimate, continuing relationship
between the living and the dead.
Like the celebration of a birthday, it
reconfirms annually the love,
goodwill, and generosity that the
beloved can count on, no matter
that they are dead."*

JUANITA GARCIAGODOY

INTRODUCTION

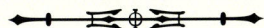

In Western cultures, we tend to perceive death as the end of the world. Unexpected and invariably tragic, it's the fate to be avoided at all costs. We cloak the occurrence in euphemisms, take a day or two off from work to attend the funeral, then try our best to buck up and move on with life. If we dwell too long on the loss of a loved one, we're deemed morbid and irrational.

Mexicans, on the other hand, not only accept the inevitability of death, they embrace its power as being essential to the fabric of life. As Octavio Paz wrote in **THE LABYRINTH OF SOLITUDE**, "The Mexican is familiar with death, jokes about it, caresses it, sleeps with it, celebrates it; it is one of his favorite toys and his most steadfast love." For them, dying isn't fatal; it's part of the continuum of time and space. They celebrate *Día de los Muertos*, Day of the Dead, an exuberant, sensual, remarkably life-affirming fiesta for the dead. The name of the holiday is actually misleading, as the ceremonies take place over three days, October 31 to November 2.

Both at home and in cemeteries, families construct elaborate altars called *ofrendas* to honor their ancestors. They adorn these altars with fragrant marigold blossoms, candles, photos, favorite foods of the deceased, candy skulls, and other symbolic items. The vibrant mix of colors, smells, flavors, and potent nostalgia are meant to lure and guide the spirits back to earth for a family reunion. Offerings are made of things that especially pleased the dead in life—tequila, rhinestone earrings, silly comic books—so that their souls may briefly delight in these pleasures once more.

This **Day of the Dead** box with its folkloric tiered altar and skeleton figurine is the start of your personal memorial *ofrenda*. To commemorate your loved ones in this way is a cathartic, soothing process which helps transform the painful mystery of death into a source of nurturing strength. To do this is to consciously and conscientiously make time to remember your dead, to hold them dear in your heart, and proclaim to the world in three-dimensional space that you loved them while they were living and you still love them now that they're gone. It is to cherish the fact that their memory sustains you.

"LIFE AND DEATH ARE NOT CONTRARY WORLDS. WE ARE A SINGLE STEM WITH TWO TWIN FLOWERS."

Juan Rulfo

ORIGINS OF THE DAY OF THE DEAD

The roots of Day of the Dead are a tangle of pre-Hispanic indigenous Mexican beliefs and post-Conquest Spanish Catholic influence.

For the Aztecs, religion and art were inextricably bound together. A central component of their religion was ritual sacrifice of human beings and animals; death imagery abounds in their sculpture, painting, architecture, and poetry.

They believed that a soul's destiny was determined not by the moral correctness of one's behavior while living, but rather by the specific cause of a person's death. People who died in battle, perished during childbirth, or were sacrificed to the gods went to a heaven called the

Dwelling Place of the Sun. If they died of drowning, dropsy, gout, or lightning, they went to Tlalocan, a heaven ruled by the rain god Tlaloc.

Infant souls went to a heaven called Chichihuacuauhco, where a wet-nurse tree fed them milk from its branches. People who died of natural causes were less fortunate. They went to a fearsome, complicated hell called Mictlán, where they had to undergo a series of trials which included trekking eight deserts and eight hills, and facing wild animals and obsidian-bladed winds. The dead were buried with goods to take with them on their metaphysical journey—food and drink, clothing, toys, pottery, arrows, and sacrificed servants.

The Aztecs celebrated two major fiestas in honor of the dead. The first, the Little Feast of the Dead, occurred in the ninth month and was dedicated to deceased children; the other, the Great Feast of the Dead, in honor of adults, took place in the tenth month. These festivals included music, dancing, and graveside offerings of flowers, *tamales*, and figurines of deities sculpted from a dough of amaranth seeds and human blood.

In Nahuatl poetry there is much consideration of the hereafter. In a pre-Hispanic poem, which is translated on the following page by Grace Lobanov and Miguel León-Portilla, the poet Ayocuan contemplates his mortality.

*Will I have to go like the
flowers that perish?
Will nothing remain of my name?
Nothing of my fame here on earth?
At least my flowers,
at least my songs!
Earth is the region of the
fleeting moment.
Is it also thus in the place where
in some way one lives?
Is there joy there, is there friendship?
Or is it only here on earth we
come to know our faces?*

DAY OF THE DEAD CEREMONIES TAKE PLACE OVER THREE DAYS, OCTOBER 31 TO NOVEMBER 2

After the Spanish Conquest of 1521, twelve Franciscan friars were charged with the spiritual conversion of the Indians. The friars burned pagan icons, destroyed sacred shrines, and imprisoned the idolaters' priests. However, because the Aztec feasts for the dead somewhat mirrored the Catholic feast days honoring All Souls and All Saints, the friars merged these holidays to facilitate the conversion process. All Souls' Day on November 1 commemorates all the faithful departed, and All Saints' Day on November 2 honors all Christian saints and martyrs, known and unknown. While the Indians observed the new holidays, many of them secretly clung to their native religion. The result is Day of the Dead, a creative fusion of Catholicism and indigenous beliefs.

A more recent influence can be found in the work of the brilliant Mexican engraver José Guadalupe Posada (1852–1913). Many contemporary Day of the Dead folk

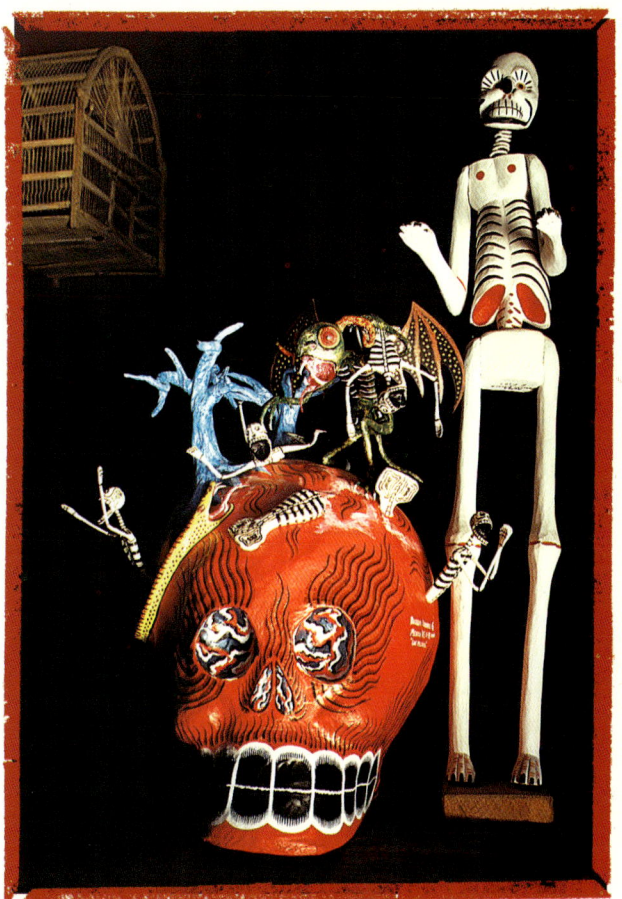

artists draw inspiration from his *calaveras* (skulls), humorous images of cavorting skeletons which illustrated popular broadsheets. These satirical verses and cartoons, often laced with social or political commentary, used skeleton characters in modern dress to mock the antics of the living. Posada's images are still popular today, especially *La Catrina*, a fancy victorian lady wearing a huge, feathered hat.

POSADA'S IMAGES ARE STILL POPULAR TODAY, ESPECIALLY *La Catrina*, A FANCY VICTORIAN LADY WEARING A HUGE, FEATHERED HAT.

To have a very good fiesta, you must use what is at hand—corn husks and turkey feathers, flour sacks and toilet paper rolls—to make Versailles. Mexican fiestas are handmade. They are sewn into being. Painted. Molded. Boiled. Cut. Every planet has to be sewn onto the sky.

❋

The pleasure of the day, its mystery, is beauty. The everyday world is transformed. The village recreates itself in beauty with cheapness and brightness. Everything is enchanting, nothing mundane. But the poignant enchantment comes from knowing that everything that is beautiful is also mundane. And will revert, when time reasserts itself.

RICHARD RODRIGUEZ

HOW THE Holiday IS *Celebrated*

Day of the Dead is one of Mexico's most passionately celebrated fiestas, equal to Christmas in its sacred importance and ritual splendor.

Contemporary Mexico is a country of nearly sixty different ethnic groups, each of which imbues the holiday with its unique customs. A Zapotec Indian teenager in rural Oaxaca might spend days helping her mother prepare the traditional offering of black *mole*, whereas a college student in industrial Monterrey might buy a bag of potato chips to place on the altar at a Day of the Dead-themed disco party.

Each year, thousands of tourists inundate the Purépecha Indian villages around Lake Pátzcuaro to see the spectacular nightlong cemetery rites. In comparison, coastal resorts such as Puerto Vallarta have scant public observance of the holiday, though most residents assemble private memorial altars in their homes.

While each region puts its distinct spin on the holiday, there are elements common to all. For instance, people of every age and from all walks of life participate in the festivities. They look forward to the season as a time to renew bonds with the dead and the living, as the celebration brings the community together to feast on special holiday foods, reminisce, joke around, and catch up on local gossip.

PREPARATIONS

Day of the Dead preparations begin months in advance. Mexico's folk artists rise to the occasion with brilliant outpourings of whimsy and ingenuity. They transform meager materials—cardboard and wire, chickpeas and glitter—into amazing objects like tiny toy skeleton circuses, complete with tinsel-eyed acrobats riding skeleton horses. Woodcrafters carve ceremonial masks, statues of saints, and crosses. Candy makers begin their labor-intensive process of molding sugar skulls and animal figures.

"WHILE LIFE YET LASTS, LAUGHTER AND MOLASSES"

Traditional Mexican Proverb

Embroiderers stitch bright new napkins. Potters begin to turn out incense burners. Candle makers dip tapers of all sizes, and farmers plant fields of marigolds to harvest for the memorial altars.

Families save up and splurge for Day of the Dead, because traditionally every element of an offering should be new. In practice, this isn't always possible, but when needed, this is the time to buy a new tablecloth or to replace chipped coffee mugs. No expenditure of money, time, or creativity is too lavish when made in honor of the dead. This is their fiesta, after all, and they deserve the best.

Particularly in rural Indian communities, the Day of the Dead fiesta is viewed as a sacred obligation. Dead souls are thought to intercede the way saints do on behalf of the living. Believers call on them to influence daily mortal concerns such as weather, romance, health, and financial prosperity. The dead protect the living, however, only if they feel properly respected. If souls don't receive their annual Day of the Dead feast, they suffer and weep and inflict punishment on the living. Children are told cautionary tales warning of the harm that comes to those who disappoint the dead. Thus offerings are both expressions of gratitude for blessings enjoyed the previous year and prayers asking for more help in the following year.

Men, women, girls and boys all pitch in with the fiesta chores—the shopping, cleaning, cooking, and altar preparations. Thousands of Mexicans working in the United States return home for the holiday. The festivities are heightened by a keen awareness that everyone eventually joins the dead. Celebrants take to heart the classic Mexican adage, "While life yet lasts, laughter and molasses."

Starting in late October, the everyday food markets swell with a dazzling array of seasonal goods. Between the butcher stalls and vegetable stands, you'll find makeshift tables with vendors selling mountains of white candles and fabulously gaudy memorial wreaths trimmed with pastel tulle, tinfoil, and Christmas bows. Trucks pull into town heaped with marigolds, cockscomb, gladiola, carnations, and baby's breath. Bakers paint merry skeletons on their windows to advertise *pan de muertos*, the special bread of the dead.

Candy makers present a menagerie of sugar figurines made of *alfeñique*, a paste of icing sugar, egg whites, lemon juice, water, and binding powder. These figures are decorated with vegetable coloring, sugar sprinkles, and sparkling dust. Placed on altars and eaten as treats, they are shaped like lambs, dogs, cats, rabbits, turtles, pigs, chickens, bulls, and angels. The handmade effigies often exude tremendous personality—gentle little lambs and

wry old felines with whiskers of blue icing. The sugar-paste artists also create miniature replicas of food offerings such as tacos and enchiladas, and craft their most popular item of all, candy skulls.

These delectable skulls adorn memorial altars and are given as gifts to children and friends. The name of the recipient is specially painted across the skull's forehead. Children gobble them up and scream for more. Lovers exchange them like valentines. It's not a strange or gruesome gesture; it's a holiday tradition. To give a candy skull is to say, in essence, "I honor your sweet spirit, whether living or dead." At the same time, to swallow a skull monogrammed with your name is to concede your mortality. It is to remember the bones buried inside your own body and, it is hoped, to treasure life more deeply as a result.

In elementary school, students observe the holiday by painting pictures of graveyards and writing poems about their ancestors. They do so with the casual nonchalance with which children in the United States reflect on Thanksgiving by drawing turkeys and pilgrim hats. The Mexican government encourages these activities to promote national identity and pride.

Children also become acquainted with death by playing with folkloric holiday toys. These imaginative knickknacks include skull mobiles and rattles, skeleton stick-puppets, and miniature coffins with pull-strings that make grinning corpses pop to life. Made from inexpensive materials such as papier mâché, clay, wood, tin cans, and cotton balls and painted fetching primary hues, these frisky skeletons are meant to entertain both live and dead youngsters, as they are placed on graves and home altars dedicated to children who have died.

Margarita Salcedo Arroyo de Fick, an esteemed cut-paper artist of Huichol Indian heritage, fondly recalls her childhood as being "full of deaths, wakes, prayers, flowers, candles, coffee, weeping, and laughter." She explains, "The cemetery came to be a very familiar place, especially on the Day of the Dead. I visited so many graves, and we decorated each one with different colored flowers. Sometimes we picnicked on the memorial stone of my mother's family. We all came together there, and we children ran around filling the flower vases with water. I remember with nostalgia the huge fountain basin carved from gray cantera stone, strategically located in the middle of the cemetery."

THE ALTAR IS OFTEN TRIMMED WITH LACELIKE TIERS OF COLORFUL CUT PAPER, CALLED *Papel Picado.*

ALTARS

According to local custom, families construct Day of the Dead home altars anywhere from two weeks to a day before October 31st. They set up a table in the main room of the house and cover it with white satin, embroidered cotton, oilcloth, or decorative paper. Boxes or crates wrapped with cloth or paper form tiers on which the offered articles are displayed. At the center of the altar they place a holy image—a cross, a prized postcard of the family's patron saint, or a statue of Christ or the Virgin of Guadalupe. Near the religious icon(s) go photos of deceased family members and friends. If portraits aren't available, as is often the case in poor villages, then a sugar skull with the departed one's name on it is used to invoke their presence.

The family gathers favorite clothing and possessions that either belonged to the dead or that have been newly purchased in the soul's honor. For a country man these items might include his sombrero, his machete, and a pack of his preferred brand of cigarettes. As with the food offerings, these things are eventually used by the living once the altar is dismantled. The family also incorporates articles that were used in the person's work, such as a musician's instrument or a fisherman's net. Sometimes

the deceased's interests are represented by humorous folk art figurines—a harried skeleton writer pounding away at a computer or a miniature skeleton bathing beauty lazing in a walnut-shell tub.

The front of the altar table and the back wall behind it are often trimmed with lacelike tiers of colorful cut paper, called *papel picado*. Perforated with a hammer and chisel, craft knives, or scissors, these many-hued banners are patterned with simple geometric shapes or more complex designs of angels, birds, churches, flowers, and fanciful skeletons. Made from tissue or metallic paper, these delicate decorations lend a joyous air to the occasion. Easily torn, they also serve as a metaphor for the impermanence of human existence.

Since Aztec times, Mexicans have honored the dead with orange marigold blossoms. They continue to beautify their memorial altars with profuse bouquets of them and sometimes also sprinkle a welcoming path of petals for the returning souls to follow from the front door to the altar. In regions where it's hard to grow flowers, blooms of plastic, paper and silk are used. Like the ephemeral cut-paper art, flowers symbolize the perishable nature of life.

Beeswax or paraffin candles are positioned both on the altar table and on the floor before it. Usually they are

THE ALTARS OFFER WHATEVER FOODS MOST PLEASED THE DEAD IN LIFE.

white, but they come in all sizes and shapes—some with paper decorations, others cone-shaped, still others poured into glass votive containers. The soft, comforting light of the candles illuminates the pictured faces of the dead, helping the living remember them. It's believed that the souls warm their cold hands over the flames.

Copal incense, made from a resinous bark, smolders on the floor in front of the altar. Its pungent blue smoke blesses the offerings. A small plate of salt serves to represent the spice of life, and a glass of pure water is set out to refresh the soul after its exhausting journey from the other world. Adding to the altar's lush vibrancy are fruits of the season: oranges, bananas, chokecherries, limes, jícamas, apples, and guavas. Strung in garlands and piled in artful arrangements, fruits bring appealing aroma and color to the composition.

Loaves of *pan de muertos* adorn the altar. This light, sweet yeast bread has many regional incarnations. In some places, it's made into round loaves and decorated with strips of dough shaped like skulls and crossbones, flowers, or teardrops; in other areas, the loaves look like little human bodies, birds or fish. The bread's glazes are equally diverse, including pink frosting, butter, orange-blossom water, and shiny egg yolks.

A cup or bottle of the honoree's favorite beverage is placed on the altar. Typical drinks include coffee, hot chocolate, fruit punch, and soda pop. *Atole*—a hot corn gruel flavored with chocolate, ground almonds, honey, cinnamon, or pureed fruits—is also popular, as are alcoholic beverages such as tequila, beer, and mezcal.

The family lovingly prepares the deceased's favorite foods in abundance. In Indian households, many of the dishes date back to the pre-Hispanic era when corn, beans, and chocolate were staples. In wealthier *mestizo* communities, the food offerings tend to include homemade traditional fare, plus more expensive commercially produced items like candy bars and cookies. The intention is the same, though: to serve whatever foods most pleased the dead in life.

The most common Day of the Dead meals are *mole* and *tamales*. Once again, there is great regional diversity in how these delicacies are prepared. Depending on the combination of chiles used in the sauce, *moles* can be red, yellow, green, or black. Hours in the making, the intense sauce requires at least a dozen herbs and spices, including, in most recipes, chocolate, as well as pureed nuts, seeds, bread, tortillas, and tomatoes. Typically it's served with turkey or chicken and comes topped with a sprinkling of toasted sesame seeds.

Tamales are made in a hundred different forms, some sweet and some savory, but all with corn as the main ingredient. They come wrapped in corn husks, banana or avocado leaves, aromatic herbs, and *agave* skins. Fillings range from mashed beans to mint-spiced pork to briny shrimp to raisins and coconut. Most varieties are steamed,

but some are baked, others simmered in broth, and still others cooked in underground pits.

Altars memorializing children usually include simpler, less spicy food. Children's souls are called *angelitos* (little angels). If a child died before he or she could hold a cup, a baby bottle full of milk is offered for the soul to drink. Bread and water are also laid out, as are treats such as chocolate, crystallized fruit pastes, and sweet pumpkin stewed in molasses. Baby's breath and white orchids are considered children's flowers. Their altars are often adorned with *papel picado* banners patterned with angels and doves. Sometimes families set up a separate altar especially for children alongside that for the adults and make all of the offerings miniature—doll house teacups, tiny breads, and thumb-sized sugar animals.

It is customary for guests to visit home altars for children on October 31 after dusk, and altars for adults the following evening, November 1. Visitors bring gifts for the dead, often bread or a candle. Guests are greeted with mugs of warm fruit punch or cinnamon-spiced hot chocolate. Some people think that souls return as doves, butterflies, dogs, and even neighbors—so on those fiesta nights, it's important to show hospitality to every living creature that crosses your path, because you never know, one of them might be your dead uncle.

THE RITUAL ISN'T ABOUT GRIEF AND SOLEMNITY; IT IS ABOUT REMEMBERING AND FEELING CLOSE TO THE DEAD.

The ambience of home altar gatherings is generally congenial and upbeat. It would be disrespectful to receive the dead with sorrow, since they've come such a long way to visit. Care is taken to make the food and drinks with especially robust flavors and smells, because the souls are thought to absorb the essence of offerings rather than physically consume them. They feast on the pungent sensory blend of flowers, fruit, incense, sugary confections, melted wax, and steaming casseroles. After the dead have their fill, the living eat, sometimes needing to add a pinch of salt, since the food isn't as flavorful after the dead have partaken of it.

GRAVESIDE

Goods from the home altar are bundled up and taken to the cemetery to make graveside offerings. In communities that hold nightlong cemetery vigils, families typically spend the afternoon of November 1st preparing the graves. Where night vigils are not the custom, families usually pay their cemetery respects the morning of November 2.

During the day, the graveyard pulsates with life as families bustle about with armfuls of candles and wheelbarrows loaded with flowers. They pull weeds and tidy up the graves, sometimes refurbishing tombs with fresh coats of paint (in classic Mexican shades like shocking pink, lime green, and electric blue). Vendors hawk balloons and *tamales*. Festive rockets explode overhead and children play hide-and-seek among the headstones. Some communities organize graveyard music and masked dance extravaganzas. The ritual isn't about grief and solemnity; it is about remembering and feeling close to the dead.

Cemetery decorations range from a few scattered petals on an unmarked grave to majestic marigold-encrusted bamboo trellises called *arcos*, which might adorn a newly deceased grandmother's tomb. A toddler's grave might be adorned with sprays of white baby's breath and a little rag

DEAD SOULS AREN'T USUALLY SEEN, BUT THEIR PRESENCE IS FELT.

doll, tenderly arranged. The most opulent decorations are reserved for the recently dead. The first year after someone dies, the family is obligated to construct as extravagant an offering as possible. The ability to make a beautiful show of respect bestows prestige on the family. Shaped as arches, hearts, or crosses, and festooned with flowers, fruit, corn, bread, candy skulls, and sugar figurines, the extravagant trellises represent the bounty of life.

The night vigils begin at midnight on November 1 with the tolling of church bells and continue through dawn on November 2. In the cold dark, the graveyard becomes a quiet sea of candles, black braids and warm *rebozos* (shawls). Smoky fires shoot sparks high into the air. The night smells of copal incense and decaying flowers.

Extended clans gather around their family plots. Each family unit brings a basket full of fruit, bread, and more candles. They place the basket, covered with embroidered

napkins, on the grave, then rip apart a bunch of marigolds, sanctifying the offering with a quick toss of petals. Some people serenade their dead with folk songs and toast to their well-being with shots of tequila. Others stare quietly into the flames and pray. Everybody takes turns playing with the many wide-awake babies. Dead souls usually aren't seen, but their presence is felt. Rather than being a séance, the night vigil is a matter-of-fact cosmic family reunion. It's simply assumed that the dead are there at the cemetery, enjoying the gossip and cooing babies along with everyone else.

MORNING AFTER

Dawn breaks, revealing all the graves to be covered with baskets, petals, and dripping candles. Families dig into their baskets and exchange plates of fruit and bread with their cousins, neighbors, and friends. When giving the food, they say, for example, "Please accept this small offering from my mother." The receiver kisses the food and says thank you, then digs out an apple or roll from his or her basket and hands it away with another, "Please accept this small offering from my great-grandfather." In this way, with gifts from each other's ancestors, everyone leaves the cemetery as they arrived, carrying a basket full of food—but the contents are not the same offerings they brought.

TRADITIONAL RECIPES

The following Day of the Dead recipes were generously shared by Arminda Flores of the Purépecha Indian village of Ihuatzio in the state of Michoacán. Arminda's mother taught her how to make these dishes when she was a child, and she in turn passed them on to her daughters, who she hopes will someday carry on the tradition with their own children.

MAKES 1 LOAF

¾ *cup lukewarm water*

2 tablespoons dry yeast

4 cups all-purpose flour, plus extra for dusting

¾ *cup plus 2 tablespoons sugar*

1 teaspoon salt

3 eggs

1 stick unsalted butter, softened to room temperature

1 teaspoon vanilla extract

❧ **PAN DE MUERTOS** ☙
Bread of the Dead

Pour the water into a small bowl and gradually stir in the yeast. Allow the yeast to proof in the water for 10 minutes.

Put the flour in a large bowl and form a well in the center. Pour the water/yeast mixture into it and mix well.

Add the sugar, salt, eggs, butter, and vanilla extract, and stir into the flour mixture. Knead the dough on a floured board, adding flour as needed until it's no longer sticky.

Butter and flour a clean bowl. Place the dough in it and cover with a cloth napkin. Leave in a warm place until the dough doubles in size, about 45–75 minutes.

Separate four-fifths of the dough. On a greased baking sheet, shape it into a round base. Form the remaining dough into 6 long teardrop shapes and 1 smooth ball. Place the ball in the center of the loaf and the teardrops in a circular pattern around it. Let rise another 90 to 120 minutes.

Bake at 400 degrees for 15 minutes, reduce heat to 350 degrees and cook until browned, about 15 more minutes. When cool, brush with melted butter.

CHOCOLATE
Mexican Hot Chocolate

The unique flavor of Mexican chocolate comes from a rich blend of toasted cocoa beans, sugar, cinnamon, vanilla, and ground almonds.

SERVES 4

1 quart milk

2 round tablets of Mexican chocolate

Heat 1 cup of milk in a pot with deep sides. When the milk is warm, add the chocolate tablets, broken into quarters. Mix with a traditional *molinillo* (a hand-carved wooden beater which you rub between your palms), or stir with a wooden spoon, until the chocolate is melted. Add the remaining milk, reduce heat, and simmer for about 2 minutes, or until heated through. Remove the pot from the heat and whip the chocolate with the *molinillo* or in a blender.

CALABAZA EN TACHA
Pumpkin Stewed in Syrup

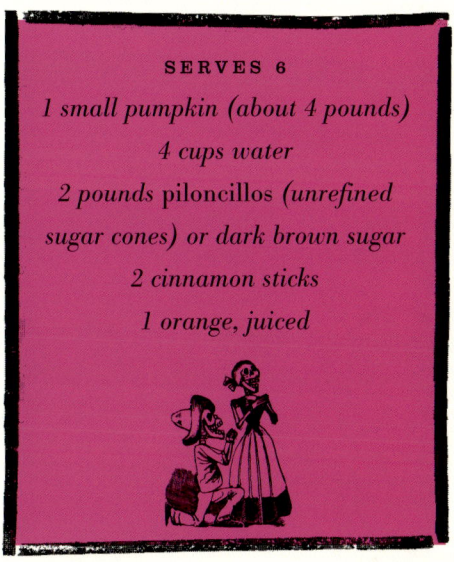

SERVES 6

1 small pumpkin (about 4 pounds)

4 cups water

2 pounds piloncillos (unrefined sugar cones) or dark brown sugar

2 cinnamon sticks

1 orange, juiced

Cut the pumpkin into chunks and discard the seeds and pulp. In a saucepan, combine the water, sugar, cinnamon sticks, and orange juice. Cook over low heat, stirring often, until the syrup thickens. Add the pumpkin, cover, and simmer over medium heat for about an hour, until the pumpkin turns a deep caramel color. Remove the pot from the heat and let the pumpkin cool in the syrup.

PONCHE DE LAS FRUTAS
Hot Fruit Punch

SERVES 25

½ cup dried jamaica *(hibiscus)*
flowers, rinsed and drained

1 orange, peeled and chopped

2 apples, cored and chopped

1 pound round yellow guavas, cut
in half and seeded

3 cinnamon sticks

10 tejocotes *(tiny crab apples)*

1 piece fresh sugar cane, chopped

2 pounds sugar

2 gallons water

Combine all ingredients in a large pot. Bring to a boil and let simmer for 1 hour.

NACATAMALES
Pork-filled Tamales

To make *tamales*, you will need to prepare *masa* (cornmeal dough), salsa, filling, and corn-husk wrappings. Note: commercially prepared *masa* or *masa harina* (flour made from dried masa), as well as dry corn husks, lard and chiles can be purchased at many Mexican grocery stores in the United States.

MAKES 16 TAMALES

MASA
(Cornmeal Dough)

2 cups masa harina

1 teaspoon baking powder

½ teaspoon salt

2 cups warm water

⅔ cup lard or shortening

To make the *masa* dough, combine the *masa harina*, baking powder and salt in a large bowl. Using a wooden spoon, slowly stir in the water to make a moist dough. In a separate bowl, beat the lard until fluffy, about 2 minutes. Add the *masa* mixture to the lard and continue to beat until a spongy consistency is reached, about 2 minutes more. Set aside.

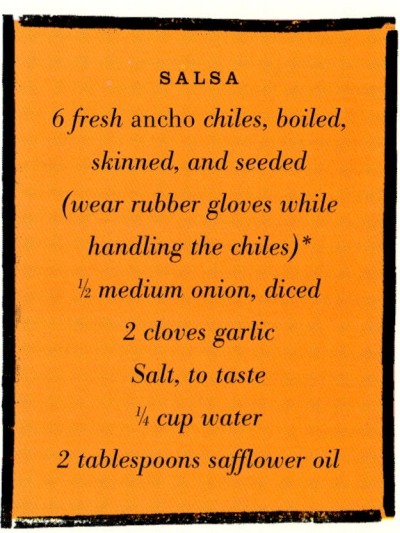

SALSA

6 fresh ancho chiles, boiled, skinned, and seeded (wear rubber gloves while handling the chiles)*

½ medium onion, diced

2 cloves garlic

Salt, to taste

¼ cup water

2 tablespoons safflower oil

To make the salsa, puree the *ancho* chiles, onion, garlic, salt and water in a blender until a smooth consistency is reached. In a non-stick saucepan, warm the safflower oil and add the salsa mixture. Cook over medium-high heat for about 5 minutes. Set aside.

* *(Note: If using dried chiles, soak in hot water for about 10 minutes before removing stems, seeds, and pureeing.)*

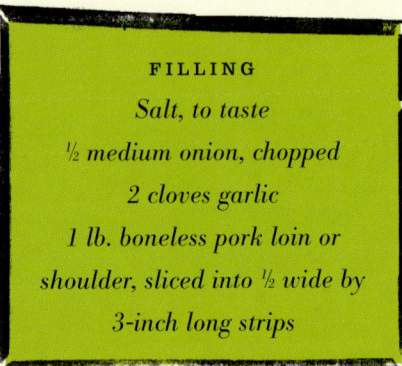

FILLING

Salt, to taste

½ medium onion, chopped

2 cloves garlic

1 lb. boneless pork loin or shoulder, sliced into ½ wide by 3-inch long strips

To make the filling, bring 3 cups of water to a boil in a medium pot. Add the salt, onion, and garlic, and bring to a boil again. Add the pork and cook until tender, about 15 minutes. Remove from the pot with a slotted spoon and set aside.

WRAPPING

16 dried corn husks

To soften the dry corn husks, soak them in a large bowl of hot water for about an hour. Remove from bowl and gently squeeze out the water.

ASSEMBLY

Finally, to assemble the *tamales*, scoop a handful of *masa* dough, layer half of it into a concave side of the corn husk, top it with a little salsa and meat, then enclose the filling with the remaining *masa*. Fold the long sides of the corn husk to the center, then fold the ends up to make an envelope. When finished stuffing the *tamales*, place them in the basket of a steamer. Place steamer over a pot of simmering water. Cover pot with a tight lid and steam for about 1 hour. Serve immediately.

"...many individuals are turning for comfort and stability to the ancient powers of objects: not the glossy consumer items we are encouraged to buy, but the priceless, tarnished relics of personal and family histories. These things represent our triumphs, our epiphanies, our tragic losses; we cherish them, display them, and endow them with magic."

JEAN M^CMANN

CREATING YOUR Day of the Dead HOME ALTAR

No matter how traditional or quirky, simple or ornate, private or public you decide to make your Day of the Dead altar, the most important thing is your loving intention. The objects you place on your altar are meant to embody the legacy of your loved ones and to entice their souls back to earth for a visit. You are encouraged to adapt the Mexican folk traditions to reflect your own heritage, taste, and spiritual beliefs.

For instance, if the person you're honoring was a sophisticated New Yorker, then by all means offer them lobster canapés and a martini instead of chicken *mole* and a shot

of tequila; assemble bouquets of red roses rather than orange marigolds; and perfume the air with Chanel No. 5 instead of copal incense. By choosing items that are personally meaningful and placing them with care, you will create an altar that is luminous with memory and its own authentic beauty.

You can use the tiered box that came with this book as a miniature altar or incorporate it as one element in a larger altar.

It can be a poignant and gratifying experience to construct a memorial altar together with relatives or friends. Inviting children to participate in the process is a wonderful opportunity to pass on family stories, fostering a vital sense of connection with ancestral roots as well as assuaging the fear of death.

❧ GETTING STARTED ☙

Decide whom you want to honor, be they lost relatives, friends, or a co-worker, teacher, or inspirational public figure. While it's not traditional to make *ofrendas* for dead animals, many of us love our pets as family members, so commemorate yours if you wish. There's no limit to the number of souls you can include on your altar.

**YOU CAN USE THE
TIERED BOX THAT CAME
WITH THIS BOOK AS
A MINIATURE ALTAR OR
INCORPORATE IT
AS ONE ELEMENT IN A
LARGER ALTAR.**

Choose the location for your altar. The traditional place for a home altar is on a living room table; in public buildings, altars are usually displayed in entryways or lobbies. Other suitable spots include dining tables, fireplace mantles, bookshelves, bedside tables, window sills, dresser tops, and chairs.

Next, choose a photograph or portrait of the honoree. Paste the image on the back wall of the altar box, prop it up on one of the tiers, or place it next to or in front of the altar box. Make a photocopy of the image if it would fit better reduced or enlarged, or if you prefer to save the original.

If you don't have access to an image, choose an object that somehow reflects the person's physical presence. For example, if your great great-grandfather was a cowboy, you could represent him with a pair of scuffed boots.

❧ YOUR OFFERINGS ❧

Think about your loved ones' passions. What gave them pleasure? What made them tick? Remember good times you shared. Did they enjoy any hobbies? What sort of work did they do?

Gather items that symbolize these memories—like a ticket stub from a concert you attended together, an autographed baseball, or a copy of a favorite novel. If they liked to sew, you could include a jar of buttons; if they gardened, a packet of seeds. Clothing and jewelry that the person wore in life are also powerful repositories of memory.

Choose as a spiritual icon an image or statue that speaks to the divine for you. It can be an archetypal religious figure or symbol, a guardian angel, an element from nature such as an amethyst crystal or a smooth river stone, or any other object of spiritual significance.

Grace your altar with an array of blazing candlesticks, candelabras, and votives: There can never be too many candles on a Day of the Dead altar. The flickering flames are thought to illuminate the soul's passage home.

Incense is customarily burned in a ceramic chalice on the floor in front of the altar to sanctify the rite. The thick aroma of the smoke adds to the dead's sensual experience.

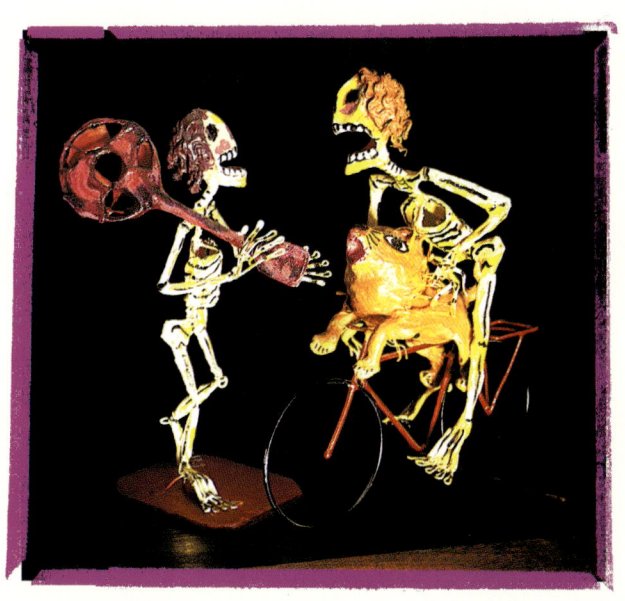

❧ DECORATIONS, FOOD, AND DRINK ❧

Traditional Day of the Dead flowers are orange marigolds, bloodred cockscomb, and lacy white baby's breath. Flowers represent the ephemeral loveliness of life. Offered on an altar, their aroma is meant to draw the dead near. Place your bouquets in whatever's handy—crystal vases or tin cans. You can weave the blossoms into a majestic arch or sprinkle petals over everything. If you like, make a path of petals leading from the front door to the altar to show the spirits which way to go.

The skeleton figurine that came with this book is a playful icon of death. Place it on your altar to help your loved ones' returning souls feel comfortable; seeing it, they'll recognize that this offering is intended for them. Other death symbols are skulls made of sugar, chocolate, or clay and *pan de muertos* (bread of the dead) fashioned in the shape of bones, tears, or little bodies.

What were your loved ones' favorite types of food and drink? Traditional *ofrendas* always include a glass of water to quench the soul's thirst after the long journey home and a little plate of salt, representing the spice of life. If you are fortunate enough to have inherited your grandmother's china, you could welcome her spirit home with an offering of tea served in her favorite cup.

THERE'S NO LIMIT TO THE NUMBER OF SOULS YOU CAN INCLUDE ON YOUR ALTAR.

Garnish your altar with fresh fruit—you can make a constellation of banana moons, orange suns, or even blueberry polka dot stars. Depending on the size of your altar, it's fine to use either symbolic, pretend food made of plastic, marzipan, or papier mâché (as designed for doll houses, refrigerator magnets, and sushi displays) or to cook a full meal. Traditionally, the spirits are encouraged to dine first, feasting on the steaming vapor of the food offering. Later, you and your friends may partake of the meal.

Move the objects around the altar until you instinctively know they're in the right place. Mexican altars are renowned for their lavish, fearless use of color. Because Day of the Dead is not a dreary event, decorate your altar table and perhaps the surrounding wall with paper cut-out

banners, confetti, streamers, balloons, stickers, satin ribbons, glitter garlands, twinkling Christmas lights, or anything else that strikes you as being festive and beautiful.

❧ HOW TO USE YOUR ALTAR ❧

To construct a Day of the Dead altar is to give thanks to those who have profoundly touched our lives. You can sit quietly at the altar, light candles and incense, and pray. You can write the souls a letter telling them what you've been up to lately. You can host a party, inviting guests to bring candles and mementos to add to the altar. Or if you feel like it, you can drink beer, crank up your loved ones' favorite tunes, and dance till dawn in their honor.

Day of the Dead altars give tangible form to our feelings of loyalty, affection, and longing for those who have passed away. The holiday isn't about ghosts and goblins; it's about the strength of family ties and enduring love. The Mexican mix of stoicism, wit, and reverence teaches us that death is a natural extension of life. By honoring our loved ones' spirits in living color, and sharing their legacies with our children and community, we nourish a sense of continuity. We are all much less alone.

"THERE IS MORE TIME THAN LIFE."

Traditional Mexican Proverb

Suggested

READING

LIST

Andrade, Mary. THROUGH THE EYES OF THE SOUL: DAY OF THE DEAD IN MEXICO. San Jose, CA: La Oferta Review Newspaper, Inc., 1996.

Carmichael, Elizabeth, and Chloë Sayer. THE SKELETON AT THE FEAST: THE DAY OF THE DEAD IN MEXICO. Austin, TX: British Museum Press and University of Texas Press, 1991.

Garciagodoy, Juanita. DIGGING THE DAYS OF THE DEAD: A READING OF MEXICO'S DÍAS DE MUERTOS. Niwot, CO: University Press of Colorado, 1998.

McMann, Jean. **Altars and Icons: Sacred Spaces In Everyday Life**. San Francisco: Chronicle Books, 1998.

Paz, Octavio. **The Labyrinth of Solitude**. New York: Grove Press, Inc., 1961.

Salvo, Dana. **Home Altars of Mexico**. Albuquerque, NM: University of New Mexico Press, 1997.

Sayer, Chloë. **Arts and Crafts of Mexico**. San Francisco: Chronicle Books, 1990.

Trenchard, Kathleen. **Mexican Papercutting: Simple Techniques for Creating Colorful Cut-Paper Projects**. Asheville, NC: Lark Books, 1998.

Winningham, Geoff. **In The Eye of the Sun: Mexican Fiestas**. New York: W.W. Norton & Company, Inc., 1997.

ACKNOWLEDGEMENTS

All photographs except those on page 20, 38–39, 44, 46–47, and 88 copyright © 2001 by Masako Takahashi. Photos on page 20 and pages 46–47 copyright © 2001 by Ed Foley. Photos on pages 38–39, 44, and 88 © 2001 by Debra Lande.

All line art by José Guadalupe Posada.

GRATEFUL ACKNOWLEDGMENT IS MADE FOR PERMISSION TO REPRINT QUOTES FROM THE FOLLOWING SOURCES:

Page 6: From **DIGGING THE DAYS OF THE DEAD: A READING OF MEXICO'S DÍAS DE MUERTOS** by Juanita Garciagodoy. Copyright © 1998 by University Press of Colorado. Reprinted with permission of University Press of Colorado.

Page 13: From **PRE-COLUMBIAN LITERATURES OF MEXICO** by Miguel León-Portilla. Translated from the Spanish by Grace Lobanov and Miguel León-Portilla. Copyright © 1969 by the University of Oklahoma Press, Norman. Reprinted by permission of the University of Oklahoma Press.

Page 18: "Introduction" by Richard Rodriguez. Copyright © 1997 by Richard Rodriguez, from **IN THE EYE OF THE SUN: MEXICAN FIESTAS** by Geoff Winningham. Used by permission of W.W. Norton & Company, Inc.

Page 68: From **ALTARS AND ICONS: SACRED SPACES IN EVERYDAY LIFE** by Jean McMann. Copyright © 1998 by Jean McMann. Reprinted with permission of Chronicle Books.

Special thanks to master paper-cutter Margarita Salcedo Arroyo de Fick in Querétaro, Qto.; to folk art maestros Manuel Jiménez in Arrazola, Oax., and papier mâché sculptors Saulo Moreno and Ricardo Linares in Mexico City, D.F.; to Betsy McNair of La Casa de Espíritus Alegres in Marfil, Gto.; to Arminda Flores and Kevin Quigley in Ihuatzio, Mich.; and to Ann Alexander, Evita Avery of La Calaca, Nancy Dusseau, Dianne Kushner of Casa Luna, Susan and Juan Carlos Ortega of La Guadalupana, Polly Stark de Ortega and CC Stark of Chaos Hecho, and Esther Ramírez of Talismán Boutique, all in San Miguel de Allende, Gto.

At Chronicle Books, we are grateful to Debra S. Lande, Carey Jones, Alethea Morrison, Elizabeth Bell, and Jodi Davis, and we thank our agents, Bonnie Nadell and Amy Rennert, for their steadfast and cheery support. We also send abrazos to Dave and Annalena Barrett, Michael Bock, Tony Cohan, Leigh Hyams, Carmen Salmerón, Nancy Gallagher Shapiro, Fred and Meg Snyder, Cilla Zweig, and to the Dear Ones.